THE HARVEST

Alban A. Olive

FEARON

The Harvest

Navan, Ontario
Canada

Published by: Rhoan Flowers' Books
Released: June, 2023

Genre: POETRY

ISBN 978-1-989995-11-2 (SC)
ISBN 978-1-989995-12-9 (EB)

Library & Archives of Canada
395 Wellington Street
Ottawa, Ontario
K1A-0N4

ANTHOLOGY

THE HARVEST

By Alban A. Olive

Pen Name: FEARON

ABOUT THE POET

Born in Grenada West Indies

Went to St Andrews Anglican Secondary School S.A.A.S.S

Awarded certificate of Merit from the ministry of culture Grenada 1978

Immigrated to Canada in 1988

ACKNOWLEDGMENTS

I want to thank my friends who encouraged me on my journey, on the road of life.

Mayann Nyack my wife, Jade Shulist, and Filip Filipovic from T.C.H.C.

Mohsin Khattak, Tasheba Queenie Gayle from Alexandra Park Resident Association

Sarah Jane Bachinski -Filmmaker and Editor

Kiley Fleming, Osopan Agie, staff from Alexandra Park Community Centre and TRIDEL.

Special thanks to many of my friends whose names were not mentioned,

You are in my heart and soul.

DEDICATION

Dedicated to my lovely mom,

Mrs. Lutha Mc Sween.

CONTENTS

YOU ARE NOT THERE

∞∞∞

When I need you

To talk to

You are not there.

When I am cold

Your loving warmness is not there,

You are like the bright daffodils in the garden.

When I need you

To hold my hands

Through the raging storm,

When my heart is full with loneliness,

When my spring is drying

And my soul is thirsty

I need you,

You are not there.

Now I am alone

On the narrow road.

WELCOME TO ALEXANDRA PARK
ATKINSON HOUSING CO OPERATIVE

∞∞∞

Atkinson co-op is one of the first

housing developments in Toronto

Boarded by four of Toronto's liveliest Streets:

Dundas Street, Bathurst Street,

Queen Street West, and Spadina Avenue.

You cannot find truth without roots
That's why roots run deep in the community.
The land which we stand on has been the site
Of human activities since time immemorial
It's the traditional territories of the
Indigenous People.

It's a multicultural community
Rich with powerful culture and history.
Do you remember Sony Atkinson
And his family roots?
Do you remember Randy Padmore and
His contribution to the community?

Today, In this twenty first century,
The community is going through
The phases of revitalization
Which uplift the community.

We are a progressive community
And we continue to prosper with our visions.
The youths are educated
With various degrees and skills
To build for the future and succeed.

We cannot forget
The beautiful Garden of Angels
With many names
Of residents who lived, contributed,
And died in the community.

Welcome
To Alexandra Park,
Welcome to Atkinson Housing Cooperative
Where roots
Run deep.

TORONTO CARIBANA

∞∞∞

Beautiful sunshine over Toronto

Smoke coming from the BBQ s

The aroma of tasty foods

Sweet calypso and socca music

Filled the atmosphere

Along the street of Lake Shore

Thousands of people

Gather together to celebrate.

Sweet calypso music

Sweet socca

With a blend of roots, rocks reggae

Let's dance and sing

Let's party and dance our waistline,

Dancing

The dance of Emancipation

In a foreign country.

Let's invoke

Calypsonian king Smokey

To come back and sing

About the pandemic disease

Named Covid-19

Keeping the masquerades jumping, screaming, and sweating

After being locked

Inside for so long.

Look!

At this beautiful mass band

Beautiful ladies, men, and children

In colored costumes.

Can you see the Queen?

Dancing graceful with her golden costume

While the King, smiling and pulling his rainbow costume

Doing the calypso dance in front of the crowd and judges.

Mister Barman, can you please give us some Caribbean strong rum?

To lighten our head, as we dance and whine

Let's celebrate

Our Carnival

It's a tribute for our Ancestors.

Caribana

It's part of our rich culture and heritage

On this land of Canada.

AT ST. MICHAEL'S HOSPITAL

∞∞∞

When you are sick

On the hospital bed

And feeling bleak

With pain

Running through your body

Call upon the Anointed One

Because He has

Your destiny in his hands.

He will be your

Spiritual Doctor

And to guide

All Doctors and Nurses

As they perform their duties.

When you are sick

On the hospital bed

With tubes carrying medicines

To your veins

To help fight the disease and ease your pains,

Remember Him, whisper his name

He will release you

From your pains.

Special thanks to Dr. Mark Wheatcroft and his team.

WORDS OF INTROSPECTION

∞∞∞

MY shadow is my friend

He is with me

Wherever I go.

....

There will be a time

When we would have to say,

"Goodbye my dear friend."

....

Love and hate

Can never be friends.

....

Where there is darkness

There is no light.

....

I meet you on my journey

On the road of life.

....

Look at yourself in the mirror

And ask yourself
Why I am here?

....

Always wear a perfect smile.

....

You look so pretty
I want to know
what lies behind
Your beautiful eyes?

....

I searched for you
Until I found you
Wisdom,
You are my best friend forever.

....

My woman is the woman
I give my crown
She is my queen.

....

Mistake made in the glorious days
Of our youth,
When not corrected
Live with you

As you grow older.

....

Marriage is like a beautiful bed
Made and blessed with sweet roses.

Be careful

Where you sleep

There maybe thorns between the roses.

....

Stop!

Smoking that cigarette

My dear friend.

....

I saw him

He is black

Black as tar,

And his dreadlocks

Is as white as snow.

....

Your sweet words

Are like honey,

To quench my thirst.

....

Here on the beach

I saw these words on the golden sands.
LOVE,
Then the tide rolls up on the beach
And carry LOVE away.

....

The absence of a father in the family tree
Is like a branch that have been cut down
From that tree.

....

As I walked by, I saw you
I am sure it is you.
I called your name
You pretend you did not hear
And continue walking.

....

The shadow of a man perish
Once his soul is gone.

....

You are young, gifted, and black
Do not throw away
Your culture.

TIME AND NATURE

∞∞∞

The black and white clock ticks
On the wall at St. Michael's hospital,
On the seventh floor at Cardinal Carter
Room sixty, bedroom one.
Below this clock, there is a beautiful painting
Its beauty shows two young children
Wearing clothes that look medieval.

The girl seat on the floor holding a rabbit
On her lap, on her blue dress,

15

While the boy
In his brown pants
Feeds the rabbits from his hands,
While the girl looks on.

Who are these two young
And happy children in this painting?
Are they siblings or friends,
Are their parents' farmers?
It seems it is the season of winter
Look!
How they dressed, feeding their pets.

The clock above continues ticking
From seconds to minutes,
Then to hours and hours changes into days
Which changes into months and months changes into
years.
It is a fact, time and nature works together
We was once young beautiful and strong
Waiting to be feed.

This picture looks ancient

The artist was once young

And perhaps died in his latter years.

In this painting

The children and their pet

Would never grow old,

Therefore, remember the glorious and happy days of your youth.

<u>COVID-19</u>

∞∞∞

We read about the Black Plague

The Spanish flu

And many infectious diseases

In the medical journals.

During our era we experience SARS and heard about
Ebola

While medical labs are still

Working to find a cure for Aids and Cancer.

Now in this year, Twenty-Twenty

In this twenty first century

There is another deadly pandemic disease

Called Covid-19.

Where did it came from

How can it be prevented?

Oh Covid-19

Dethroning all other diseases

And capturing the throne.

He ruled dangerously, traveling from country

to country,

His hosts is mankind

Have no respect for statues; rich or poor,

Black or white.

It stop the flow of citizens and immigrants and other supplies

Bringing nations economies to their feet

And changing social ways of life universally.

Many frontline doctors, nurses, and others

Become the statistics of Covid-19,

There's light at the end of the tunnel

Scientists knows some of its symptoms

And ways of preventing and controlling its spread.

Like wearing masks, washing your hands, and limiting crowds gathering

As they try to develop a vaccine.

FORWARD EVER

∞∞∞

Because we have a black president

You are thinking, dressing like a ninja

And causing trouble around the towns

No, my brothers and sisters

Because we have a black president

You are thinking, treating whites differently,

No, brothers and sisters.

Emancipate yourself from mental slavery

Look forward

Towards the twenty first century

Educate yourself, your families, and the communities,

And keep positive

With the reality of nature and history.

Because we have President Barack Obama

You are still thinking of the past days of slavery

The oppressions, exploitations, anger, and separations

That was forced upon your ancestors

You said, it's not over

Because many blood have been spilled as sacrifices.

The future looks bright

Can you see the shining light?

Because we have a black president

You want to pick up your guns

And kill the children's of the oppressors

No, my brothers and sisters.

We have to unite

And know our rights

Let's revolutionize our minds

And shake off the chains and shackles,

As we walk

On the road of life, with history.

<u>COUSIN KEN -Elegy</u>

∞∞∞

The leaves fall to the ground

The snow melts and returns to the earth

I know cousin Ken would not be around,

He is dead

He died before the welcome sun

Climb the sky.

Days before he died

He said, "I have the Big C...Cancer"

He was so young and adventurous

We used to call him 'Comparo'

When he smiles, I can see

His father's countenance.

His life was such a sweet reality

He makes everyone in his company feel happy

But I know as mankind mature

There is a time to live

And there is a time to die.

I know and you all know

Life is a glorious adventure

I cherish the moments we have spent

In this life

Mankind must find

The secret, how to live and love.

It's crying time again, weeping and mourning

We will surely miss you

You was like a shining light on the hill

We remember the kind things you did,

Here we are, the survivors,

Like birds of one feather, singing goodbye hymns.

SINGING UNDER THE APPLE TREE

∞∞∞

I heard him

Singing, singing under the apple tree

How can you say

You love me

When you have my loving heart

In the darkness of captivity?

How can you love me

When you are seeing him?

How can you love me

When every weekend, you want to party

With your friends?

How can you love me

When you are playing

Those Jezebel games?

How can you love me

When you are telling your friends

I don't love him?

How can you love me

When you are saying

I don't have enough money?

How can you love me

When you don't reason with me?

How can you love me

When you are wishing for me to die

So you can collect parts of the insurance pie?

How can you love me

When don't you like my family tree?

How can you love me

When don't you love yourself?

How can I love you

When you believe,

There is no God?

I heard him,

Singing, singing under the apple tree.

LEAPERS HILL

∞∞∞

My name is Gasoman,

From the Carib generation

Who once lived,

On the beautiful Island of Grenada in the Caribbean.

We love fishing in our canoes,

We love farming,

Cultivating sweet potatoes, yams, plantains, and cassa-
vas,

We also hunt armadillos and iguanas.

Under the moonlight sky

We gather together,

Around the bright fire.

We sang and played games

The chiefs and elders dance,

Singing and chanting praises

To our God.

We was living in peace and harmony

On our island.

Surprisingly!

One bright sunny morning

Far, far away in the ocean

We saw strange ships,

Sailing towards our island.

It was the French who anchored and came ashore,

After years living on the island

Words started to spread throughout our villages,

The chiefs and elders said,

They want to enslave us.

One day, war start on the island

The French army attacked.

Boom boom, bang bang

Bang, boom, boom, boom

Strange sounds, we never heard

Coming from their smoking guns.

For days we fought, guerilla style fighting

With our bows and poisonous arrows

Because we know the nature of our mountainous land.

On the north side of the island

On the steep hill, overlooking the sea,

We gather together.

We decided,

Instead of being slaves

We leaped

Hundreds of feet into the deep sea.

GOING HOME

∞∞∞

On Friday morning

He left the rehab

As an amputee.

His family and friends would be there

Waiting patiently

When he step out of the car

With his walker.

They would cheer and greet

And welcome daddy back home

After being away for so long.

He would tell about his experiences

During his rehabilitation

Learning to walk again, like a baby

And exercising in the gym to get stronger.

Oh! What a terrible feeling to be hospitalized

During a pandemic, named Covid 19.

With no families and friends to visit

It is isolating,

There is no summer to enjoy.

Every day and night he prays

Every day and night he says thanks

To the health care workers who take care of him.

Oh! Such a terrible disease

That strikes like a bolt of lightning,

That changes some of his future plans.

But God save his life

He will continue to be physically, mentally, and spiritually strong.

Welcome back, daddy.

IN PRISON

∞∞∞∞

Why do you cry

When you know you did commit the crime?

When you are in prison

You are not free.

You feel so embarrassed

Feeling the police fingers searching your ass,

You have to go to bed

At a schedule time,

You have to line up for your bath,

You trade apples for cigarettes.

You are in bright orange uniforms

In hand cuffs

When going to court,

You are with criminals

In the patty wagon,

And you wonder about the judges

And your sentencing.

Grey walls stand as soldiers

Around the cells,

While you wait patiently to use the phone

And watch TV and play games in the dormitory.

You hear prisoners chatting

About why they are here

And some saying, they don't care

It is better to be here.

My brothers and sisters

Who are in captivity,

Why reoffend,

Rather than reform?

When you are in prison

You are not free.

GOODBYE TOBACCO

∞∞∞

Goodbye, my friend

Good bye, Tobacco.

You are my lines

We meet in my youth

I hold on to you as a friend,

Not knowing you would become my foe

As I grow and mature.

Now in this twenty first century

As I grow older,

One thing I could not understand

About you.

Why do you have so many names?

Rothmans, Players Light, Benson and Hedge, Marlboro,

Three Fives, Next

And many more names.

I remember in history

In the early centuries

The change from sugar cane cultivations

To tobacco on many of the Caribbean plantations.

It was like a financial revolution

Rich farmers and merchants

Aristocrats and poor people

Embrace you,

Because of your blend, taste, and addiction.

You are a traveller

Roaming the earth.

Today

Nations spend millions of dollars

Educating the society about you.

Millions of dollars have been paid

By cigarettes companies to settle lawsuits,

Because you are a culprit

Causing the deadly disease named Cancer.

Goodbye, Tobacco

Goodbye, Cigarettes.

MYSTERIES

∞∞∞

In this world of life and mysteries

What have to be, have to be

You can't stop it,

You can't stop the welcome rain from falling

Neither the sun from shining,

You can't change the night into day

As we journey on life ways,

You can't change the colour of one skin

We have to accept our fellow beings,

Reality is there to see

You can't stop life with all of its mysteries.

Then you surrender

To the to the things you can stop,

From the light of the body

Reality is facts

You can surrender yourself.

See the changes of life

From the windows of your eyes

In this world of life and mysteries.

No one knows the time when they'll die

No! You can't stop it

It's mankind destiny.

WRITING FROM A FATHER

∞∞∞

My sons and daughters

This is the writing from your father

Who's blessed by the Creator.

Sons of my sons

Daughters of my daughters

Respect the instructions from the Creator

And always love your mother and father.

Sons and daughters

Without a mother and a father

You would not be on this earth,

To grow and mature to know

What life is worth.

My sons and daughters

We take care of you

From a baby to a youth

You are our seeds and roots,

We watch you grow with care, like a tree

Now we are a happy family.

There are many stages in life

Be careful, strong and do not give up hopes,

You will mature

With the positive teachings of life

And you will know as you grow

What is wrong and what is right.

Living in this world of changes

Don't forget your history

In this world of trials and tribulations.

Remember to seek the Creator

And you will be blessed

And rewarded, with love forever

To continue the cycle of life.

When I return to my Creator

Physically I would not be around,

Remember my positive teachings

And hold on to wisdom, knowledge, and understanding.

SHE IS SLEEPING

∞∞∞

Sleep! My love sleep

In your sleep

You look so beautiful

Beautiful as the Queen of Sheba.

My lover, my woman

I can feel the warmth breathe of air

As you exhale and inhale

While you lay motionless

After your daily works is completed.

My beauty

My lover

Is dreaming,

Maybe dreaming about us

Holding hands and talking

As we walk slowly in the park,

Or maybe dreaming of entering

In the kingdom of New Jerusalem

That she read and heard about.

Sleep sweet, my dear

Oh sleep!

You are a mystic.

My lover will awake

When he awake her,

I looked at her eyes again

Before going back to sleep

In my heart and soul, I said to myself

Who can find a virtuous woman

And make her his wife,

And to grow old together?

IT'S A WOMAN WORLD

International Women Day-Tribute

∞∞∞

The late James Brown sang

It's a man world .

Stating all the earthly things

Men does and achieve,

But how can we forget

Those great women

From the days of creation

Who help build many nations!

Today, it's not a man's world

Equality, in the sight of God.

Women have more love

They embraced and nurse babies

And does cooking, cleaning, and laundries,

While men sit on the couch

Drinking beers and watching T.V.

Be realistic

Let's recognized

It's a woman's world.

They are strong

They goes through many trials and tribulations.

Men should find a virtuous woman

To grow old

And to enjoy the beauty of creation.

Do you remember the history

Of Cleopatra and the Queen of Sheba?

Do you remember Rosa Park and Viola Desmond?

Do you remember these powerful words,

'Woman behold your son'

And I saw Him, he is risen'.

Oh Woman

Mother of Christ

You are heroes.

And today,

We celebrate,

Standing on their shoulders of life.

Those women who paved the way

As legends

It's a woman's world.

A MAN WITH A VISION

Dedicated to Adam Vaughn from Residents of Alexandra Park

∞∞∞

May God bless your parents

Wherever they may be

In your heart, they are happy and free

In your glorious youth

They inspired you

To search for the truth.

Now you are a man

A family man

Continuing your mission

With your visions.

I remember those glorious days

Those journalistic shining rays

Which uplift, to higher heights,

Telling the truth to the nations.

Travelling on the road

Of trials and tribulations

With wisdom, knowledge and understanding,

You are a gifted politician,

You are the people chosen champion,

With your strength and gifted heart

From roots you knows

The sociology of the communities

We wish you the best, on your journey.

WISDOM

∞∞∞

The fear of the Lord is the begging of wisdom

And the knowledge of the holy is understanding.

In my youth

I search for wisdom

Instead I find knowledge and understanding.

Now I am older

I continue searching for you

Wisdom!

You are my best friend

You are my bride and I am your groom

I will always be with you

Because you are true

You are more precious than rubles.

For the lord giveth wisdom

Out of his mouth cometh knowledge and understand-
ing

Happy is the man that finders wisdom;

And the man that getteth understanding

For the merchandise of it is better

Than the merchandise of silver,

And the gain thereof than fine gold.

Wisdom is the principal thing;

Therefore get wisdom;

And with all thy getting get understanding.

Exalt her and she shall promote thee

Take fast hold of instructions

Let her not go, keep her for she is thy life.

HAND IN HAND

∞∞∞

We black people

must walk with pride

I see poor people

Walking after iniquity

And they all speak lies

Shout!

Oh Israel! and rejoice

With all thy hearts

Let's not thine hands be slack.

Captivity road my friend

Leads to burden

Oh! Daughters and sons of Ethiopia

The days of wrath

Is the days of trouble

All this days have gone away

Long, gather ourselves together

Oh! Black people

Come! Let's make a move

We must walk hand in hand.

THIS NOOSE

∞∞∞

Please! Remove this noose

From his neck

It's getting tighter and tighter

He could hardly breath

Please! Cut him loose

From this terrible noose.

Why do you put him

In a noose?

Is it because he knows

His ancestors roots?

Or is it he knows

The truth about suffering?

He could hardly breath

His feet floats, inches from the ground

His eyes cry the tears of suffering

He is innocent mortal being.

In this life, he tried his best

Walking in the shadows of love, peace, and happiness

Like the wind, changing direction

Could you change your mind

And cut him loose

From this terrible, historical noose.

SOCIAL LIVING

∞∞∞

Life is full of stages
And there are many authors
Who have a place in the universe
Because of the creators plan.

But the best of all
Are understanding, knowledge and wisdom
Giving but the creator
As he made man to fulfil his missions.

I love social living because it's inspiring
To the average human being
Social living is like a running stream
And truly, its experiences is a glorious feeling.

Living in the universe socially
Is full of experiences and philosophies

Listen to the conscious men of arts

Their experiences must have facts.

THE HARVEST

∞∞∞

I can see the welcome sun

Rising in the distance

As I pray, I know it's the beginning

Of a new day.

It is such a long time

since Jesus Christ left

It is such a long time

Since African slaves came to the plantations.

I know God is watching his children

Let's praise the king of kings

Because he went to prepare a place

For his chosen race.

We are the survivors

Let's have courage and faith

Like farmers,

Waiting to harvest their crops,

While men harvest, the harvest of proscription.

AFRICAN ROOTS

∞∞∞

Africa! Africa!

Land of black man culture

A beautiful continent

We must always remember,

Our ancestors

In chains as slaves,

Shipped across the oceans

To strange plantations,

Whip! Whip!

Work! Work!

Hardly any rest,

After toiling and toiling

Their masters harvested the best.

Africa! Africa!

Your famous history

Would never die!

WELCOME

∞∞∞

Welcome!

To my heart

Welcome!

To the house

That is built

With loyalty

Endurance and perseverance

Welcome!

To my heart

Built with love.

FROM THE ROCK

∞∞∞

May your soul rest in peace

My dear friend

Harrison Philip

"The Rock"

On our discussion on the BIBLE

He said,

"B is for BELIVE

I is for its INSTRUCTIONS

B is for BEFORE

L is for LIVING

E is for EARTH"

Believe in its instructions before

Leaving earth

That's his philosophy of the bible.

YOU ARE GONE

∞∞∞

I thought, I was your only lover

I thought, I was your only woman

I know our love was strong

But, I was wrong

Now you are gone

With another woman.

I cried, many teardrops

Days and nights,

When I realize our love

Was not right.

I gave you, my loving heart and soul

hoping we would be together

When we grow old

Not knowing, that was not your goal

Now you are gone

Gone with another woman.

YOUNG LOVE

∞∞∞

The moon is gone
my love
let's awake our love light
And bring some light
Into our life

So young is our love
So old is the night
Feeling your tender
Arms around me
You make me feel happy

Cirrus clouds fade away
Our love is here to stay soon,
You would be on your way
After enjoying your summer holiday!

<u>BEAUTIFUL GRENADA</u>

∞∞∞

There is an island in the Caribbean

In the West Indies

Which captures my heart and soul

Beautiful Grenada! Conception Island, Isle of Spice,

I love you.

I will always remember you,

In my childhood days

Playing games in the sun, in the rain

And in the moonlight .

Beautiful Grenada

Your majestic green mountains,

Golden Grand Anse beach and Bath-way

Together with other characteristics

Add to your beauty.

As we grow and mature

Our school days was educating,

Learning of many subjects and topics

And our historical and cultural heritage.

We love you

Grenada

We would never forget our heroes

T.A Marryshow, Uriah's Butler, Julien Fedon, Maurice Bishop, and Eric Gairy.

We would never forget

The citizens who struggle daily

To uplift the development of the nation.

My dear friends

These are my poetic lines

I am a patriot.

There are so much to see and know

Would you like to visit

The Island of Spice.

DEMONSTRATIONS AND EXE- CUTIONS IN GRENADA

DEDICATED TO THE SURVIVORS WHO EXPE- RIENCE THE FALL OF THE GRENADA REVO- LUTION

AND THE COMING OF THE AMERICAN, BRITISH, AND CARIBBEAN MILITARY FORC- ES.

∞∞∞∞

Reading of history

And civilization

While travelling on creation

Men make history

And history makes humanity famous.

I surely remember

In the town of St. George's,

On fort George

Red flowing blood

Runs like streams on the ground.

Reading of Grenada history

In this century,

In the year 1983

Patriotic citizens together with

Prime minister Maurice Bishop

And members of his Revolutionary Government

Spill blood to the ground

Red dripping blood

Red flowing blood.

GO AWAY RACISM

∞∞∞

It is said," We came from

The Dark Continent "

We are proud

Proud Africans.

Proud of our rich land, history, and cultures

Why do you want to uplift

The teachings of Racism

Mr. Professor?

Can you see, we are Humans

Blessed by the Creator.

You said, "We are inferior "

Do you know, it's a sin

In the eyes of the Creator?

You know

Mankind was made by the Creator.

With your education and qualifications

Spiritual values,

You fail to find.

Your theories on Racism

Is causing problems on this land.

While we are praying

For the death of Racism

You are teaching indoctrination.

HE SOLD HIS SOUL TO THE DEVIL

∞∞∞

My grandmother used to tell us stories

About men who wanted to become rich

By following the devil philosophies.

One moonlight night, she said to us

There was this handsome rich man

Who lived in the village,

One night, in the dead of the night

He called his son and said

'Son let's go out for a while'

Not asking any question

He decided to obey his father command.

They got into the truck

And his daddy drove straight to the nearby beach

And parked abruptly

He switched off the lights and said to his son

"Wait for me here"

And walk away in the darkness.

One hour passed as he looks at his watch

He became frightened

Because his daddy parked the truck

Facing the roaring sea and taking so long to return

Therefore, he decided to turn the truck around.

And waited behind the driver seat in the dark

He heard a trotting horse

So he looks back

And saw a huge black horse

With his daddy sitting on its back

Coming towards him.

He starts the engine and turns on the lights

And speed towards his home,

He told his mom what happened

She said, "Son daddy is in the room"

When they went and looked,

Daddy is dead on the bed.

The villagers said,

"Because he didn't sacrifice

His son to the Devil

He is dead instead!"

NEGLECT THE TEACHING OF LIFE

∞∞∞

GOD said," Let there be light "

And there was light.

Shining bright, in the garden of Eden

When you are living

In the dark

There's no light

To brighten your life.

Wisdom, knowledge, and understanding

Have been taken away from you

Because you are not true.

There you sit

On the throne of darkness

Ruling, with the philosophies

Of ungodliness.

ANCESTORS VILLAGE

∞∞∞

One rainy night
In dreamland
God said to me,
"My friend,
Come walk with me
To see your Ancestors village."

My brothers and sisters,
Children of my children,
Here we are
On this very high hill,
Looking!
At this village.

Beautiful valleys,
Beautiful green gigantic trees
Pointing towards the sky,
Swinging with the breeze
On this beautiful dawn.

Rivers and tributaries
Meanders towards the sea,
Acres of sugar cane plantations
Stretching as far as the eyes can see.
Fields of cassavas and plantains
Add to its glory.

Smoke from small huts
Climb slowly to the sky,
Flocks of different birds
Sing as they flapped by,
While the majestic rising sun
Paints pictures across the sky.

I can see the ancient sugar mill
With gigantic wheels,

Slowly rotating with history
Men, women, and children
Happily cultivating the fields,
Fishermen with canoes on the beautiful beach
With their catchers of the day.

Then I turned around
To asked Him,
"God,
Where's this land
And village?"
He was gone.

IN DREAMLAND

∞∞∞

This morning my friend said to me,
"Last night in dreamland
I meet this beautiful woman
At a club in Toronto
We danced all night long
To many beautiful songs
On the ballroom floor."

She said, "I am from Barrie,
I came downtown
With my girlfriends to party
And now you are with me
I feel free
Like a blue jay
In the trees,"

She said, "After the party
We would drive

To Barrie

To meet my family."

It was love and affection

When I awake

I realize, I was in dreamland.

EMANCIPATION WOMAN

∞∞∞

Born on the first day of August
Born free with love
It's a gift for your parents
Your birthday is on a great day
A historical day, called Emancipation Day.
Now you are a senior woman
Looking strong as the rock of Gibraltar
You are like a fortress and well protected
Because of your spiritual belief.
You stand majestically with your white locks
While your black face shines in the morning sun.
You spring from the roots of slavery
Your ancestors were here, hundreds of years ago.
And today
Your generations stand on your strong shoulders.
You inherited lands from your ancestors
You are not so rich and not so poor
Your wealth is your glorious health.

Today you stand in your latter years
With your children and grandchildren
Physically and spiritually strong
Always praising the great God.

MOONLIGHT

∞∞∞

Tonight, the moon is shining

My love

Shining bright with all its glory

In the month of August

And here we are

Looking through the glass windows

On this beautiful summer night.

Sitting in the heaven

Like a king on his throne

Dressed with majestic glory.

It's the beauty of art

Created by the Creator,

With his artistic brushes

He paints the natural rays of light with nature

This moon, still carry its glory and duties

From the beginning of time

And tonight

Thousands of stars hanging majestically

As protective soldiers in the heaven.

There he sit, in all of his majestic glory

Controlling universal climates, humanity moods

And the seasons of the years.

SPEAK THE TRUTH

∞∞∞

When I was a child

My grandparents and parents

Always used to say, "Speak the truth!"

And "Be careful little tongue, what you say."

Now I grown to become a man

I truly understand.

The tongue is one of humanity dangerous weapon

The deceitful words from one tongue

Can put many in trouble.

While the immoral words from one tongue

Comes back and sting like a bee,

Always speak and preach the truth from your heart and
soul.

Even though you may be persecuted

The truth is like an everlasting spring

Which never runs dry.

It clenches your thirst like sweet honey combs

And nourishes your memories with wisdom,

Knowledge, and understanding to survive in this peril-
ous times.

Many people from different nationality and culture

Have been persecuted and imprisoned

For speaking and preaching the truth.

Remember in the days of old during the Romans rule

Jesus Christ was crucified, and John pays the price with
his head,

Yet his disciples and apostles continue preaching the
truth.

Saint John the Divine was imprisoned

While others was killed and persecuted.

Throughout history

Generations comes and generations goes,

While the truth never die

It's immortal.

Beware! There are false leaders and preachers
Who misled their followers from the truth,
Through the teachings of indoctrination
Which at times leads to massive murders,
Like Jim Jones in the jungle
On the South American colony of Guyana.

Throughout history
There are many facts of truth,
Too numerous to mention in my poetry.
There is a scripture which says,
"I am the way the truth and the light "
Seek the truth, the truth never die.

IN THE BACK YARD

∞∞∞

Here I am in the back yard

Listening a flock of birds on the trees feeding on insects

Suddenly! Here comes a hawk

And scoop up a bird

In its powerful claws

And fly away.

I look in the corner of the wall

And there's a spider

Spinning its webs

Here comes two flies

And flew in its web,

The smaller one get stuck

While the bigger one flew away.

Early this morning, on the history channel

I saw a lizard feeding on flies,

Slowly a snake crawls up

And eat the lizard.

The worms crawls up from the ground

And the birds ate the worms,

The parson eats the birds

And the red fox eat the parson.

The bear kill the fox

And worms feed on its carcass.

Life in the wild is hard

Only the strongest survives.

YOU ARE MY MOTHER

∞∞∞

You are my Mother

I know you are my Mother

You are from creation,

Tell me! Do you have

A dear Mother

Who is as beautiful

As your first lover?

Mother's love

Is such a sweet reality

Her tender touch

Makes me feel happy.

You had the power

To abort me

You said, no

Life is such a sweet reality.

Tell me!

Do you have a dear Mother,

Who you cherish

Not only on Mothers Day?

CULTURE

∞∞∞

Culture is the artistic manifestation

Which characterizes a society.

Culture makes you free

When you understand the sociology of a community.

One without the knowledge

Of their culture

Is like a dying rose

In the flower garden.

Culture brings nations together

Through the seven forms of art,

Nourish your cultural heritage

In this world

Of material

And cosmopolitan attitudes.

MOTHER EARTH

∞∞∞

This is the land

Our Ancestors toiled

From the beginning of creation,

The land is a secret heritage

For the born and unborn

From generation to generations.

This is the land

With its majestic glory

This is the land

That was given by the Father.

This is the land

Mankind have to return,

This is the land

Let's cherish Mother Earth.

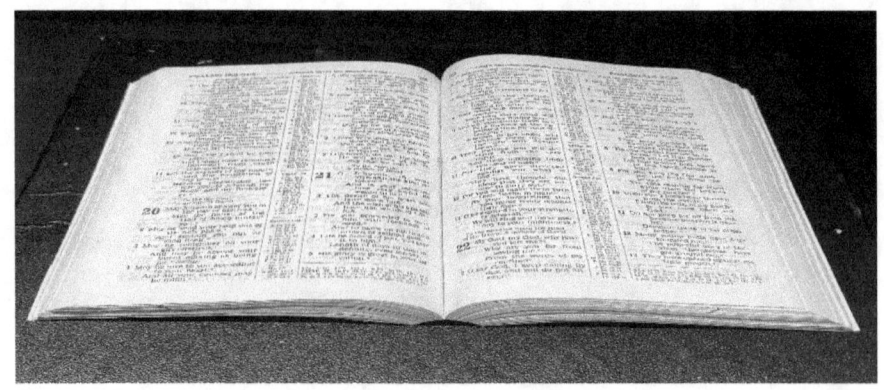

CHANT A PSALM

∞∞∞

I can hear the welcome rain falling

This morning

Here I am

Reading and chanting.

It's such a powerful and spiritual feeling

Learning from my God and King

I lift up my eyes to the hills

From whence does my help come from?

My help comes from the Lord

Who makes Heaven and Earth'.

As I read and chant

From the book of Psalms

King David was gifted with everything

Blessed with wisdom, knowledge, and understanding.

'The Lord is my Shepherd'

In this foreign land,

As I travel with guidance

And protection in Babylon.

'Blessed is the Man, who walks not

In the counsels of the wicked'.

When Satan and the wicked are raging

I chant some Psalms,

From your spring I drink

To nourish my heart and soul.

Oh! Ancient King

Your poetic verses

Makes me feel happy and free

On this rainy morning.

SATAN

∞∞∞

The Prince of Darkness

Live in the tower

Built with ungodliness

With his servants

Having their titles

Named Sin.

Roaming the earth

Deceiving human being

With their ungodly

Philosophies and doctrines.

THE TRIAL OF JESUS CHRIST

∞∞∞

I read in the Bible

About the trial of Jesus Christ

Thousands of people gathered to see

The persecution of this great man

Including his disciple Peter

Who denied knowing his Master.

Pontius Pilate, the man in charge

Remember the dream his wife had,

About this man.

He asked Christ, "Are you the King of the Jews?"

Pilate knew Christ won

Because he asked and answered,

His own question

And as a symbol, he washed his hands.

LOVE NEVER DIE

∞∞∞

Love is the blooming of the red roses

In the flower garden

Love is looking at yourself in the mirror

And saying to yourself, I love you.

Love is the fresh breadth of air

At dawn,

Love is that beautiful sound

When couples said, I do.

Love is that beautiful smile

When we look at each other eyes.

Love is that bright light

Coming from the welcome sun,

Love is chanting psalms

Of praises to the King of Kings,

Love is embracing

Wisdom, knowledge, and understanding.

UNITED TOGETHER ITS NOT OVER

Dedicated to the doctors, and health care workers and the survivors of Covid 19.

∞∞∞∞

Comrades

No turning back on the narrow road of life

Like soldiers carefully advancing towards their foes

With all their ammunitions

Advancing to the dangerous front lines.

Together they are united

With a common goal

Staying positive and alive,

All those years of training

Is the blueprints of their mission

Where theory changes into practical

And life is not fantasy

Life is reality

We have to battle this terrible disease.

Then we look beyond our third eye

And put on their uniforms

And try to walk in their boots,

Laced with faith and courage and felt scared

Then undressed ourselves from this mortal garments

And drift towards the back line.

How many can stand firm

Advancing to the front line with their comrades

With heart beating, with no fear

Singing silently

We shall be victorious.

When the war on Covid 19 is over

We would be living heroines and heroes

Because we have fought a great battle.

We would celebrate

We would weep and mourn,

For our friends and family

Who becomes victims of Covid 19.

We would dance and sing,

We would praise Him,

We would sing the lyrics.

One love,

Because we have captured

Covid 19.

BIG MEN DON'T CRY

∞∞∞

There is an old saying

"Big men don't cry "

When faced with the reality of life.

I can say, that's a lie

Why do mortal men

Cry these teardrops from their eyes?

History states Jesus Christ

Wept on the cross,

And you are saying

Big men don't cry.

I saw him crying in the corner

With his brother,

After his girlfriend boarded the airplane

And wave a lengthy goodbye.

There is an old saying

"Big men don't cry "

I saw him look at the judge,

Embraced his lawyer

And cry

Knowing there is limited freedom

Behind prison walls.

I saw a father crying on City T.V.

His best friend, his son died

By a stray bullet in the BBQ party.

Do you remember

During President Obama inauguration?

I saw Rev. Jessie Jackson between the crowd

Crying,

Knowing he live to see the first black president.

There is an old saying,

"Big men don't cry "

I saw him cry after he was baptized

Knowing he would have to walk

The narrow path to paradise.

And you are still saying,

"Big men don't cry."

TRUE FRIENDS

∞∞∞

The poor is disliked

Even by his neighbours

But the rich has many friends,

Grandma used to say

"Show me your friends and

I will tell you who you are."

True friends are like diamonds

That are rare to find.

True friends stick together

Through all types of weather,

With loyalty, respect, and commitment.

True friendship is like a chain

Whose links remain unbreakable.

True friends stand together

Like Shedrock, Mishop, and Abendigo

Like in the days of old.

In sickness, health, and death

True friends respect

Each other culture, religion, and belief.

THERE IS A CHANGE

∞∞∞

Granny since you left

There is a change in this country,

August came and said goodbye

Hurricane Allan

Destroyed parts of the Caribbean

And we had a Revolution.

Grandma

There are beautiful roses

In your lovely flowers garden,

Honeybees suck nectar

From the blossoming flowers,

But love

Still lives home.

THE CROSS

∞∞∞

History records the Romans

Made Jesus carry His cross

To be crucified

One of his friend tried to help him

But was pushed aside

By angry Roman soldiers

Imagine his physical pains

With tears and sweat

Running down his sorrowful face

While blood rushes through his wounds.

Everyone have to carry

Their own cross

Humanity can't run away

From this fact

Humanity have to choose

What is right

From what is wrong to live

In this world of trials and tribulations

Some people pray to God

To remove this unseen cross from their back.

In life

Things don't come easy

It's part of mankind destiny

Jesus carry His cross

So that mankind can be free

Physically, mentally, and spiritually

Therefore,

Be strong, humble, and wise

As you carry your cross

With endurance and perseverance.

MENTOR

∞∞∞

You are my mentor

Upon your solid rock

I build my foundation

For my generation.

You are my mentor

I will hold on to you forever.

You uplifted my soul

With your spiritual teaching.

You are my mentor

A father figure.

No more dark clouds in my path

Your philosophies of life is my light.

TEACH ME HOW TO PRAY

∞∞∞

They sit around the dining table

He said, "Thank you mom

For these varieties of food

You prepared for supper,

And thank you

Dear God for this wonderful meal!"

He said, "Mommy can you teach me

How to pray

So, when I am older

I would never forget the Creator

And thanking HIM
For our daily meals."

I know God gave mommy
The enduring strength
So she can work
Put food on the table
And pay the bills and rent
As a single parent

He said to his mother,
"I saw some starving children on TV
They look so innocent
Their crying eyes
Cry the tears of bitter hunger
In this humid refugee camps!"

Oh! how I wish they were like me
Where their mommy can put food
On the table and pray over their meals
It seems only death

Can free them

From their miseries.

IT'S A BEAUTIFUL DAY

∞∞∞

It's a beautiful day

Glorious sunshine,

The bell peel from the church,

Birds singing in the maple trees,

Light breeze blowing from the east,

Pigeons feeding in the park,

Babies are born

Breathing the breath of life,

While their daddy and mommy

Enjoy their gift of love.

On this beautiful day

Peace would be made,

Goals would be set,

Progress would be made,

Dreams would be fulfilled,

The living would bury their dead,

As the clock ticks

On this beautiful day.

Oh! What a beautiful day

The farmers prepare their crops,

Let's give praises,

To the Creator

And His followers,

Who preaches the truth daily

Oh! What a beautiful day!

THE TALKING DRUM

Black History, everyday is Black History Day

∞∞∞

I hear the sounds

Of the talking drums

Far away

Coming from the Asanti tribes

On the African land of Ghana.

With wood, animal's skin, and skills

They make these beautiful drums

Just as their ancestors did

Many, many years ago

As part of their rich cultural heritage.

And here I am

On this land of Canada

Listening to the talking drums on television

And understanding the Ashanti's historical documenta-
ry

In this twenty first century.

I can hear their powerful sounds

It is sweet music to the ear, heart, and soul

There are different sounds for peace and war

Sounds for birth and sounds for death

There are sounds for people to celebrate and get to-
gether.

Each drum beat and sounds

Send a message of belonging

Imagine, in the days of old

Without televisions, radios, and phones

Today, the talking drums is still the historical means of
communication.

MY CREATOR

I love you

From my heart and soul

I will continue loving you

When I grow old

Without the breath of air

I would not be here

Without love

I would be long gone.

Thank you for having me on this land

And protecting me

From the teachings of Satan,

Although you are spiritual

You remain my God and King.

Through struggles and happiness

You never forsake me,

You always shines Your light

As a guiding path

On my journey.

Reflections of life

In the days of old,

Stand as a testament

In this modern days.

I love you

From my heart and soul.

BLACK WOMAN

∞∞∞∞

Black

Beautiful

Black woman

I believe

Love pulled his bow

And open the door

To your heart.

Life is so mysterious

Love is so adventurous

Cirrus clouds fades away

Here we are

On this beautiful day.

Black

My sweet

Black woman.

SPEAK TONGUE SPEAK

∞∞∞

Like a trumpet, echoing sound and power... Speak

Tongue speak you are not dumb... Speak

You are free

Speak with the freedom of words

Don't be afraid to speak

Like the prophets of old.

Let your chosen words be true

And pure like a spring of clear water

So, one can drink and digest

From the spring of knowledge... Speak

Tongue speak, it's your gift

Don't be afraid to speak

About the oppressions and unemployment on the land

And the corruptions done by some politicians

And men in high positions.

Come on tongue... Speak

About the Beast in the book of Revelation

And his false witnesses

Preaching words of deceits... Speak

Tongue speak,

About the dangerous drugs on the streets

And its danger to society... Speak,

About poverty and people living in tents

Lack of affordable housing, high rent

In the cities and the fear of Covid 19... Speak

Tongue speak

You have the sound and power,

Let's give praises to the Creator

Thanking Him

For the breath of life

While we are still here... Speak,

Tongue speak!

THE BLIND SINGER

∞∞∞∞

She is so young

And she is blind

Not seeing the light

From the rising sun

Neither the faces of her Parents.

The way she sing

She brought light

Into her life,

You are young and beautiful

With a gifted voice.

You sing from your heart and soul

You make the audience

Cheering and dance

To the lyrics of your songs.

You are a young genius,

Your sight is your voice

You remind me of the great legends

Stevie Wonder and Ray Charles.

HE KEEP SEARCHING

∞∞∞

I saw him

On the Murry's show,

He doesn't know

His father

He doesn't know

His mother.

He is in his late thirties

And he keep searching,

He is disappointed

The man he embraced with love

As a father,

Was not his daddy.

Tears roll down his face

As they embraced,

His heart is in pain

Knowing he have to keep searching again.

THE PROPHET

∞∞∞∞

ISAIAH wrote

"Oh, house of Jacob

Come let us walk

In the light of the Lord."

To be a Prophet

Is a profit

For Jehovah,

The Prophets came

People lets rejoice and sing

Spiritual songs and hymns

For our God and King.

In visions

The Master reveals His plans

For the Prophets

To tell to the Nations

On the road of Creation.

STRANGE SHIP

∞∞∞

Here I sit

On the sandy beach

Watching a strange ship

Far, far away

In the deep blue sea

With tall white spars

Pointing towards the heaven.

In my solitude

I remember

The terrible days of slavery.

Did you sail to ports of Africa

Where my ancestors

Were kidnapped and shackled

And carry to the new world?

Here I am

Alone,

On the sandy beach

Watching a strange ship,

Then dark rainy clouds

Came along the horizon

And obscure my vision.

Am I dreaming,

Or seeing a ghost slave ship

From the days of old

As I sit on the beach?

<u>WINTER</u>

∞∞∞

I can see many leaves

Falling to the ground

Some trees stand naked

As a newborn

The mornings and evenings

Becomes darker

It's wintertime again.

Summer is gone

Some birds migrated

Squirrels live deep down in the trees

While colonies of ants

123

Borrowed deep down

In the earth.

The wind blows cold

And the homeless man

Curls in his sleeping bag

At the corner of the intersection.

Oh winter!

You are so cold

You are a part of nature's history

Snow in the country

Snow in the city

Look!

Over yonder

Groups of homeless men and women

Hurrying,

Going to the shelter.

MENTAL HEALTH WELLBEING

∞∞∞

When you are feeling

Down and depressed

Do not give up

Try to think positive

It helps to keep the mind

Healthy, strong, and active.

I still love you

∞∞∞

It's been many years

Since you are gone

I have your beautiful picture

Hanging on the wall.

Your smile are like blossoming roses

In the lovely flowers garden

Your eyes shines like the welcome sun

Across the horizon.

I surely miss you every day

As I travel along life way

It's been many years

Since you are gone.

SIMPLICITY

∞∞∞

Simplicity is my Lady

Awake! Simplicity and let's walk

The narrow road

Let's greet the creative morning with humility

Draw!

From the fountain of love

Can you behold nature

Blessed by His Majesty?

Drink!

Open your mouth

And drink from the spring of Love

Simplicity, we are no strangers

We are compatible.

Come!

Let's pray for the creative

Given Love

Let's drink!

From the cup of eternity

Can you feel the early dawn of peace

Blessed with patience?

Simplicity,

Be realistic,

Love.

Welcome to Alexandra Park Atkinson Housing Co-operative

Atkinson Co-op is one of the first social
housing developments in Toronto
Bordered by four of Toronto's liveliest streets:
Dundas Street, Bathurst Street,
Queen Street West and Spadina Avenue.

You cannot find truth without roots
That's why roots run deep in the community.
The land which we stand on has been the site
of human activities since time immemorial
It's the traditional territories of the
Indigenous peoples.

It's a multicultural community
Rich with powerful culture and history.
Do you remember Sonny Atkinson
and his family roots?
Do you remember Randy Padmore and
his contribution to the community?

Today
In this twenty-first century
The community is going through
The phases of revitalization
Which uplift the community.

We are a progressive community
And continue to prosper with our visions.
The youths are educated
With various degrees and skills
To build for the future and to succeed.

We cannot forget
The beautiful Garden of Angels
With many names
Of residents who lived, contributed
And died in the community.

Welcome
To Alexandra Park
Welcome to Atkinson Housing Co-operative
Where roots
Run deep.

- Alban Olive

Alban Olive, poet

Alban Olive came to Canada from Grenada in 1988 and
has been living in Alexandra Park for 17 years. Alban is
known as a charismatic, passionate resident leader
serving on the Board of Directors of the Alexandra Park
Residents Association (APRA), the Alexandra Park
Community Centre (APCC) Steering Committee, and
the Revitalization Working Group. A poet for over 30
years, Alban is proud to share his deep appreciation and
love for Alexandra Park's unique past, present and future
with the people of Toronto.

Savannah Lavallée, artist

Savannah Lavallée is a multi-media artist who grew up
in Atkinson Co-op. This piece, a visual response to Alban
Olive's poem "Welcome to Alexandra Park Atkinson
Housing Co-operative," is a reflection of the unchanging
aspect of a neighbourhood - its people - through their
day-to-day activities. The digital artwork explores the
daily lives and contributions of a community living and
thriving through change. Resilience is a key strength of
those who set down roots in the community and Savannah
sought to capture this through vignettes of her memories
of her neighbours' lived experiences.

Engagement with Alexandra Park youth and the
Revitalization Working Group was a key source of
inspiration for the ideas and imagery represented in
the artwork.

Savannah Lavallée's work is heavily inspired by her
insights as a Black woman living in downtown Toronto.
In addition to digital art, Savannah has created paintings,
illustrations and other art using gouache, oil paints, alcohol
markers, canvas, wood and many other materials.

Savannah is grateful to the local service providers that
have supported her and connected her to the
programming, training and arts creation/facilitation
opportunities that have played such an important part
in the growth of her artistic practice. These agencies
and organizations include the Alexandra Park Community
Centre, St. Stephen's Community House, Scadding Court
Community Centre, Central Tech High School, Oasis
Skateboard Factory, Whippersnapper Gallery and
the AGO.

Savannah would like to thank Toronto Community Housing
and Tridel for the opportunity to create and showcase
this mural in the community she calls home.

Follow or connect with Savannah on Instagram at
@sava.lava.art

THE END

www.ingramcontent.com/pod-product-compliance
Lightning Source LLC
Chambersburg PA
CBHW071157120626
46546CB00006B/2306

* 9 7 8 1 9 8 9 9 9 5 1 1 2 *